3

Tough Faith Questions

Participant's Guide

Other Resources by Lee Strobel

The Case for Christ

The Case for Christ audio

The Case for Christ—Student Edition (with Jane Vogel)

The Case for Christmas

The Case for a Creator

The Case for a Creator audio

The Case for Creator—Student Edition (with Jane Vogel)

The Case for Easter

The Case for Faith

The Case for Faith audio

The Case for Faith—Student Edition (with Jane Vogel)

Experiencing the Passion of Jesus (with Garry Poole)

God's Outrageous Claims

Inside the Mind of Unchurched Harry and Mary

Surviving a Spiritual Mismatch in Marriage
        (with Leslie Strobel)

Surviving a Spiritual Mismatch in Marriage audio

What Jesus Would Say

Other Resources by Garry Poole

The Complete Book of Questions

Seeker Small Groups

The Three Habits of Highly Contagious Christians

In the Tough Questions Series:

Don't All Religions Lead to God?

How Could God Allow Suffering and Evil?

How Does Anyone Know God Exists?

Why Become a Christian?

Tough Questions Leader's Guide (with Judson Poling)

3

Tough Faith Questions

Participant's Guide

Four Sessions on Forgiveness, Pain and Suffering,
the Trinity, and Islam

Lee Strobel and Garry Poole

GRAND RAPIDS, MICHIGAN 49530 USA

WILLOW
Willow Creek Resources

ZONDERVAN.COM/
AUTHORTRACKER

ZONDERVAN™

Tough Faith Questions Participant's Guide
Copyright © 2006 by Lee Strobel and Rocket Pictures
Requests for information should be addressed to:
Zondervan, *Grand Rapids, Michigan 49530*

ISBN-10: 0-310-26856-7

ISBN-13: 978-0-310-26856-7

All Scripture quotations, unless otherwise indicated, are taken from the *Holy Bible: New International Version*®. NIV®. Copyright © 1973, 1978, 1984 by International Bible Society. Used by permission of Zondervan. All rights reserved.

The website addresses recommended throughout this book are offered as a resource to you. These websites are not intended in any way to be or imply an endorsement on the part of Zondervan, nor do we vouch for their content for the life of this book.

Interior design by Angela Moulter

Printed in the United States of America

06 07 08 09 10 11 12 • 10 9 8 7 6 5 4 3 2 1

Contents

*Special thanks to Ann Kroeker and Laura Allen
for their outstanding writing and editing contributions.
Their creative insights and suggestions
took these guides to the next level.*

Preface

The idea came to me in the shower one morning: why not create a television program in which people of various beliefs—from Muslims to Christians to atheists to New Agers—could debate the most provocative spiritual and moral issues of the day?

What's more, prominent religious leaders could be invited on the program to be cross-examined about the stickiest questions concerning their faith.

Thanks to the vision and creativity of Jim Berger and Joni Holder, we ended up producing *Faith Under Fire*™ for a national television network. As predicted, the weekly show generated a slew of vociferous letters from viewers around the country. More than one person admitted that he found himself shouting back at his TV set.

This curriculum is based on the interviews and debates we aired on the program. You'll see knowledgeable and passionate experts discussing not just *what* they believe, but *why* they believe it. Our hope is that your group will provide a safe environment for you to be able to share your own thoughts and opinions—as well as to consider the viewpoints of others.

You'll quickly see that many of the claims made by the experts are mutually exclusive. In other words, the Christian and Muslim cannot both be right if the Bible claims Jesus is the Son of God and the Koran asserts that he's not divine but merely a prophet. One of them might be correct, or both of them could be in error, but each one of them cannot be true at the same time.

That's why we insist that our experts back up their claims. Can they defend their position logically? Do they have evidence from history or science that supports their assertions? Our task should be to determine where the evidence points.

In a similar way, the U.S. Constitution provides equal protection to all expressions of faith, and yet that doesn't mean all religious claims are equally true. According to the U.S. Supreme Court, the American ideal is to create a "marketplace of ideas" in which various opinions and beliefs can freely battle with each other so that truth will ultimately prevail.

So what is "true" about God, about Jesus, and about the afterlife? What can we know with confidence about issues of faith and morality? I hope you'll grapple with these issues in unhindered debate and discussion in your group.

One thing is true for sure: a lot hinges on the outcome.

Lee Strobel

SESSION
1

Is Anything
Beyond
Forgiveness?

Read It!

Keeping Score?

I wonder if God bothers to keep track of how well human beings perform here on earth. If he does, it seems like he would need a massive computer with sophisticated software to help him remember how we're doing. Maybe he uses a point system to track sins. If that's the case, he's probably got a complex mathematical formula to calculate all the trouble we cause.

So what's God's scheme? Maybe something like this: There are little sins—can they even be counted as *real* sins?—like telling a white lie to make someone feel better about her bad hair day or sharing a bit of gossip picked up at the water cooler to satisfy someone's curiosity. No one seems too alarmed by these indiscretions—there's no harm done here. The tracking system might assign only a few points to those "mistakes." Let's say they get a 1 or 2. You're only in trouble when you get a lot of them piled up over time.

The points start to add up more quickly with weightier sins. Think back to when you lied to your seventh-grade teacher to get out of detention, peeked at Sally Goodman's test answers during Chemistry, or stole a candy bar from the soccer snack bar. Those should get more points than a white lie. Let's say you earn 10, 12, or 14 points for those.

Then there are those arguable sins, the things that one person sees as a sin and another person laughs about as nothing. What about eating ten more crab legs at the all-you-can-eat seafood buffet, even though you weren't hungry: One person calls it gluttony —35 points?—while someone else calls it a great deal for the money—no points, only calories!

You called someone a name that shouldn't be repeated in mixed company. You noticed that the person felt wounded. What do you think, maybe a 56? But then if you were to actually hit or punch a person, how much worse would that be? 62 points? Unless you're boxing, of course—that's zero.

Then there are the big ones. How about stealing stuff worth over a thousand dollars? What about sleeping with someone else's husband? Are those in the upper 90s? They'd better be!

What about murder? How many points represent a life? Nothing less than a thousand points in my book.

Then again, maybe God should add another scale to track all the good things we do to bring our points down. It would be only fair—just like our court system, where we pay our debt to society by reimbursing for damages or doing time according to the enormity of our crime. Maybe if we sing Christmas carols at the nursing home, we bring our total down 10 points. Volunteer at a soup kitchen and watch the number drop 20 points. Smile at someone for 2, maybe 3 if that person smiles back. Move to Africa and work for a volunteer relief organization for a whopping 90 points per year.

It would be cool if we could simply do some kind of penance for our wrongdoings and hopefully bring those points down low enough to earn our way back into God's favor. How low do our points have to be to be good enough? Wow, if it has to be zero, we should really get busy.

Of course, as convenient as a point system would be, maybe it doesn't work like that at all. Maybe we have to feel really, really sorry, then beg and plead for God's forgiveness, all the while hoping that he's in a really, really good mood when we ask.

Or, wouldn't it be nice if God just completely forgave us, once and for all, whether we asked him to or not? That would be great, for me. I mean, I hope it doesn't work that way for Hitler, or my high school English teacher who gave me a D on my paper just because I was a week late—after all, creativity takes time. Maybe some people should have to work a little harder at earning forgiveness, but I like that system for me.

I wonder if God would ever be so loving, so kind, to offer us forgiveness with no strings attached, no points to redeem? Yep, now that would be *real* good.

Watch It!

Use the following space to take notes as you view the video in which Lee Strobel interviews Dr. Henry Cloud, clinical psychologist and bestselling author of *Boundaries, Changes That Heal*, and *Nine Things You Simply Must Do to Succeed in Love and Life*, and Father Frank Pavone, a prominent Roman Catholic priest, head of Priests for Life, and coauthor of *Rachel, Weep No More: How Divine Mercy Heals the Effects of Abortion.*

Discuss It!

1 Which is more difficult: to unconditionally forgive or to humbly ask for forgiveness? Why is forgiveness sometimes so hard for people to extend or receive?

2 What is your reaction to the idea that God forgives what human beings find unforgivable? Why is this concept hard to grasp or accept?

3 Father Pavone believes that God's forgiveness is not automatic, but rather it comes to those who repent and once true repentance is in place, there is no sin that God is unwilling to forgive. Do you believe people need to ask God for forgiveness in order to be forgiven or are they forgiven whether they ask for it or not? Explain your response.

> "The symbol of the religion of Jesus is the cross, not the scales."
>
> **British pastor John Stott**

> "Forgiveness is the answer to the child's dream of a miracle by which what is broken is made whole again, what is soiled is again made clean."
>
> **Nobel Prize–winning statesman Dag Hammarskjold**

4 Why would God refuse to forgive someone with an unrepentant heart? How is this similar or dissimilar to human forgiveness?

5 Both Father Pavone and Dr. Cloud believe that if Adolf Hitler were to have confessed his sins and asked God for forgiveness for the Holocaust, God would have wiped his slate clean. What is your reaction to that claim? Is God's mercy too great? Why or why not?

6 David Berkowitz, the "son of Sam" serial killer serving life in prison, now claims to be a Christian. On what basis do you think he is or is not forgiven? Explain your response.

7 To what extent do you believe God is willing to forgive people for the wrong that they do? In other words, is God willing to forgive everything, no matter what, or are there limits to what he is willing to forgive and forget?

8 Henry Cloud claims that because God himself, in the form of Jesus, died for our sins, the size of the payment was enormous enough to cover every possible sin. Do you agree or disagree with this claim? Why?

Watch It!

Use the following space to take notes as Lee Strobel continues to interview Dr. Henry Cloud and Father Frank Pavone.

Discuss It!

9 What do you believe it means to repent? Does repentance begin with a *decision* or an *action*? Explain. How is repentance different from simply feeling badly about one's misdeeds or just saying "I'm sorry"?

10 What's the difference between a person who expects or demands forgiveness and a person who is sincerely sorry and genuinely asks for forgiveness?

11 Dr. Cloud warns that God's forgiveness is not "cheap"; in other words, people shouldn't attempt to take advantage of God's grace by thinking they can commit whatever sins they want and God will just forgive them. Do you agree with this line of reasoning? Why or why not? What's to prevent someone from saying: "I can do anything I want, God will forgive me no matter what"?

"Look once again to Jesus Christ in his death upon the cross. Look and try to understand that what he did and suffered, he did and suffered for you, for me, for us all. He carried our sin, our captivity and our suffering, and did not carry it in vain. He carried it away."

Theologian Karl Barth

12 According to the following verses, to what extent do you think the Bible teaches that we *earn* God's forgiveness? What exactly must we do to receive God's forgiveness?

For it is by grace you have been saved, through faith — and this not from yourselves, it is the gift of God — not by works, so that no one can boast. (Ephesians 2:8 – 9)

Repent, then, and turn to God, so that your sins may be wiped out, that times of refreshing may come from the Lord. (Acts 3:19)

"The time has come," he said. "The kingdom of God is near. Repent and believe the good news!" (Mark 1:15)

If we confess our sins, he is faithful and just and will forgive us our sins and purify us from all unrighteousness. (1 John 1:9)

If you confess with your mouth, "Jesus is Lord," and believe in your heart that God raised him from the dead, you will be saved. For it is with your heart that you believe and are justified, and it is with your mouth that you confess and are saved. (Romans 10:9 – 10)

13 Father Pavone suggests that blasphemy of the Holy Spirit, the one unforgivable sin, is refusing to repent. Cloud says that the unforgivable sin is refusing God's offer of forgiveness through Jesus Christ. What do you understand the unforgivable sin to be? Why would our rejection of God's offer of forgiveness through the death of his Son be unforgivable?

Watch It! *Lee's Perspective*

One of the most profound and breathtaking teachings of the Bible is that God offers complete and total forgiveness as a gift to anyone who seeks it in repentance and faith. Sometimes people think God's forgiveness is limited or small, because they mistakenly think his clemency is like human forgiveness. But clearly it's not:

- People are often reluctant to forgive, but Psalm 86:5 says, "You are forgiving and good, O Lord, abounding in love to all who call to you."
- People forgive but don't forget, yet Isaiah 43:25 says, "I, even I, am he who blots out your transgressions, for my own sake, and remembers your sins no more."
- People forgive minor annoyances but sometimes refuse to pardon major hurts. But Isaiah 1:18 assures us, "Though your sins are like scarlet, they shall be as white as snow; though they are red as crimson, they shall be like wool."

- People put conditions on their forgiveness. But Isaiah 55:7 says, "Let the wicked forsake his way and the evil man his thoughts. Let him turn to the LORD, and he will have mercy on him, and to our God, for he will freely pardon."
- People may forgive one or two mistakes, but then draw the line. However, Lamentations 3:21–23 says, "Yet this I call to mind and therefore I have hope: Because of the LORD's great love we are not consumed, for his compassions never fail. They are new every morning; great is your faithfulness."
- People forgive but hold a grudge. "For I will forgive their wickedness," the Lord said in Jeremiah 31:34, "and will remember their sins no more."

Throughout history, the size of people's sin has never been the issue with God; the issue has always been whether people were willing to humble themselves and come clean with him about their guilt.

Personally, I can't help but love a God like that.

Chart It!

At this point in your spiritual journey, what do you believe about God's forgiveness? On a scale from one to ten, place an X near the spot and phrase that best describes you. Share your selection with the rest of the group and give reasons for placing your X where you did.

1	2	3	4	5	6	7	8	9	10
I'm not convinced that God has forgiven me.				I'm unsure what to believe about God's willingness or ability to forgive me.					I'm convinced that God has forgiven me through the payment Jesus made on my behalf.

Study It!

Take some time later this week to check out what the Bible teaches about God's forgiveness.

✦ Luke 15:3 – 7
✦ John 1:12
✦ John 3:1 – 18
✦ Acts 26:20
✦ Ephesians 1:3 – 8
✦ Ephesians 2:1 – 5
✦ 2 Timothy 1:8 – 10
✦ Titus 3:3 – 8

Why Does
God Allow Pain
and Suffering?

Read It!

Had Enough?

"My name is Brenda, and I have had a hard life, filled with chaos, turmoil, and pain. I know other people have gone through horrible things much worse than I have, but this is my life. The words I use won't come close to fully describing all that I've gone through. You merely read these words, but I lived them.

"To say that my mother was a paranoid schizophrenic is hard enough, but to have actually grown up in her household was a nightmare. To tell you that my husband was an alcoholic for twenty years is one thing, but to have actually lived in that environment is quite another. But I'm getting ahead of myself.

"I was born in the Midwest. When I was six weeks old, my mom and dad separated, so I never knew my dad. I saw him on only two or three occasions. My parents divorced when I was two.

"When I was three years old, I was molested by a neighbor. When I was four, I was molested by a relative, and at the age of eight, I was molested again, this time by another relative. To this day, I have haunting pictures of these horrible things flowing through my mind.

"When I was ten, my mother was diagnosed with paranoid schizophrenia. She was hospitalized for six weeks and given shock treatments. Her memory was affected, and when she came home she didn't remember my name. Sometimes she would wake up in the middle of the night screaming. One time, when she was really sick, she couldn't speak for months.

"Because of the situation at home, I started dating when I was thirteen—too young, I know—and at the age of fifteen, I found myself pregnant. I lost the baby at six months—she only lived four hours. I got married at nineteen and had a son. The next year, I had a daughter.

"In September 1971, my husband, a truck driver, had a serious accident. He was in the hospital for a month in a body cast. He couldn't work for a year and we were on welfare.

"After his recovery, I followed my intuition one night and discovered his semi parked behind a bowling alley. When I opened the cab door I caught him having sex with a woman. I forgave him. I thought, *I have two little kids; I can get through this.* It's not easy when you know your husband is having an affair, but when you *see* it, well, it's very hard to endure. He promised not to do it again, but that didn't hold true. Things just got worse, so I decided to get a divorce and find a job.

"Later, I married again. My second husband had five children, and we had one child together. I basically raised the children alone, because he was an alcoholic. It was a rough road. Before we married I knew he drank, but I didn't know it was this bad.

"Our marriage was in constant turmoil. I can remember checking on him one night—my woman's intuition again—and sure enough, there he was, in the pickup truck with a woman. I filed for divorce.

"One summer, there was a tragedy with a little girl who lived across the street. She was friends with my kids. She was going to spend the night with us. She came in the house as I was making dinner. She said, 'I need to go back home and put my puppy back in the yard.' I should have said, 'No, sit down and eat. Dinner's ready, you can do it later.' Instead, I let her go.

"As she crossed the street, she was hit by a car and killed. I always felt responsible. Her parents ended up getting a divorce—this was their baby. I stayed in touch with her mother for a long time, because when you go through something like that you're connected for life. That was really hard.

"My father and mother had been divorced for years. They both died on the same day in 1999—ironically, it was their wedding anniversary. Then in 2001, my son suffered a head injury in an accident at his job site. To this day, he's in a persistent vegetative state. I visit him daily and take care of him. He constantly has infections and illnesses. When I walk in his room and say his name, he'll close his eyes so I know he's in there, but he's trapped. He hears my voice, and I know he knows.

"I've dealt with this for four years. People say, 'Why don't you take him off life support and let him go?' But he can breathe on his own right now, so that wouldn't be enough. I'd have to take him off the feeding tube, and that's something I can't do.

"When I didn't think things in my life could get any worse, my daughter was found dead in her bed the day after Mother's Day. She was only thirty-seven. We have no idea what she died from. The autopsy came back with no answers. The toxicology report was inconclusive. We will probably never have any real closure. She left four children.

"These last four years—with the loss of my children—have been the worst. I'm stressed, worried, and worn out. When I look back on my life, though, I have to admit that a lot of the hardship I brought on myself by the poor choices I've made. It's like a chain reaction. I used to tell my children and grandchildren, 'Just think carefully about the choices you make. Everything you do in your life—every single decision means so much.'

"I have one daughter left now. She just turned thirty. She has two girls and a new baby boy. They are beautiful and healthy. She had her baby a week early, thankfully, because a week later, her stepsister died. Now there is little joy with this new baby—you lose a life, you gain a life. It will take a while before she gets over this most recent loss. She feels like something evil is all around us. With her sister dying and her brother's accident, she's wondering if she's next—we're all terrified.

"I know everybody goes through difficulties—life is hard, very hard. But this is what I've experienced. I wonder where God has been through all this. Did I push him out of the way, or did he leave on his own? Either way, I don't sense that he's been around much. And yet, I guess down deep in my heart I know that he's been there for me. He had to be or I would never have survived. Never. I'm just hoping that it's all over now. Is that asking too much?"

Watch It!

Use the following space to take notes as you view the video in which Lee Strobel interviews Julia Sweeney—Catholic-turned-atheist; actress, writer, and producer of a one-woman show called "Letting Go of God"; and a veteran of *Saturday Night Live* (known best for her role as the androgynous character Pat)—and Craig Detweiler, a graduate of both the USC Film School and Fuller Seminary. He's also the author of *Matrix of Meanings: Finding God in Pop Culture.*

Discuss It!

1 If God is so good and so powerful, why do you think he allows so much pain and suffering in this world?

2 Some atheists believe that the mere existence of pain and suffering in our world strongly suggests that there really is no God. Do you agree? Why or why not?

3 In what ways can you relate to the following words written by the Old Testament prophet Habakkuk? Share a personal experience you have had with pain or suffering that caused you to doubt the *existence* or the *goodness* of God.

> *How long, O LORD, must I call for help, but you do not listen? Or cry out to you, "Violence!" but you do not save? Why do you make me look at injustice? Why do you tolerate wrong? Destruction and violence are before me; there is strife, and conflict abounds.... Your eyes are too pure to look on evil; you cannot tolerate wrong. Why then do you tolerate the treacherous? Why are you silent while the wicked swallow up those more righteous than themselves? (Habakkuk 1:2 – 3, 13)*

> "Either God wants to abolish evil, and cannot; or he can, but does not want to; or he cannot and does not want to. If he wants to, but cannot, he is impotent. If he can, but does not want to, he is wicked. But, if God both can and wants to abolish evil, then how comes evil in the world?"
>
> **Epicurus, 350 BC**

4 At one point Sweeney believed that God put us here on the earth but he did not involve himself with us very much. To what extent do you believe God is involved in our lives here on earth? Give reasons for your response.

> "God whispers to us in our pleasures, speaks to us in our conscience, but shouts to us in our pains. Suffering is God's megaphone to rouse a deaf world."
>
> **C. S. Lewis**

5 Craig Detweiler claims pain and suffering is a test of character. How do you respond to this claim? What is the point of pain? Does pain exist for a reason? Are there any possible benefits from pain and suffering?

"Babies are born with multiple birth defects. Genetic disorders plague many of us. An earthquake levels a city, and thousands lose their lives in the rubble. The Bible teaches that there is not always a one-to-one correspondence between sin and suffering. When we human beings told God to shove off, he partially honored our request. Nature began to revolt. The earth was cursed. Genetic breakdown and disease began. Pain and death became a part of the human experience. The good creation was marred. We live in an unjust world. We are born into a world made chaotic and unfair by a humanity in revolt against its Creator."

Cliffe Knechtle, *Give Me an Answer*

6 In what ways does pain and suffering push you away from God? In what ways does pain and suffering have the capacity to draw you closer to God?

"The Lord is close to the brokenhearted and saves those who are crushed in spirit."

Psalm 34:18

Watch It!

Use the following space to take notes as Lee Strobel continues to interview Julia Sweeney and Craig Detweiler.

Discuss It!

7 If God has the power to end human suffering right now, why doesn't he do it?

8 Lee Strobel suggests that it's impossible to create a world with free will and not allow the possibility of pain and suffering. In other words, God cannot create human beings with a total ability to freely make meaningful choices and at the same time control them so they always make good choices. Do you agree with this logic? Why or why not?

> "Believing God is the sovereign creator and in control of the world doesn't mean He is directly, causally connected with everything that happens on this earth. He doesn't make the decision to reach down and shake loose a rock to start every avalanche. When some people hear this kind of thinking, they get nervous. They think I'm limiting God. I'm not. But I am saying God doesn't ordinarily interfere with the natural course of the universe any more often than He directly interferes with man's choices."
>
> **Jay Kesler,** *Making Life Make Sense*

9 Do you consider your freedom to choose to be a good gift from God? Why or why not? What would human relationships be like without free will?

10 If you could eliminate all evil, suffering, and sin (wrongdoing) in your life by giving up your free will, would you do it? Explain.

11 If there were no sin or wrongdoing in the world, do you think there would be any suffering and evil? Why or why not?

> "So how do theists respond to arguments like this? They say there is a reason for evil, but it is a mystery. Well, let me tell you this: I'm actually one hundred feet tall even though I only appear to be six feet tall. You ask me for proof of this. I have a simple answer: it's a mystery. Just accept my word for it on faith. And that's just the logic theists use in their discussions of evil."
>
> **Atheist Quentin Smith**

> "For whatever reason God chose to make man as he is — limited and suffering and subject to sorrows and death — he had the honesty and courage to take his own medicine. Whatever game he is playing with his creation, he has kept his own rules and played fair. He can exact nothing from man that he has not exacted from himself. He has himself gone through the whole of human experience, from the trivial irritations of family life and the cramping restrictions of hard work and lack of money, to the worst horrors of pain and humiliation, defeat, and death. When he was a man, he played the man. He was born in poverty and he died in disgrace and thought it well worthwhile."
>
> **Dorothy Sayers**

12 Do you believe in an afterlife free of pain and suffering? Why or why not?

13 Revelation 21:4 says, "He will wipe every tear from their eyes. There will be no more death or mourning or crying or pain, for the old order of things has passed away." Does it bring you any comfort to know that in the afterlife God will put an end to all pain and suffering and evil? Why or why not?

Watch It!   *Lee's Perspective*

I remember interviewing Peter Kreeft, a Catholic philosopher at Boston College, about pain and suffering for my book *The Case for Faith*. "There's no question that the existence of evil is one argument against God," he told me. "But in one of my books I summarize twenty arguments that point persuasively in the other direction, in favor of the existence of God. Atheists must answer all twenty arguments; theists must only answer one."

I agree that the evidence of science and history build a powerful case for God's existence. At the same time, I can understand when people undergo emotional or physical pain and begin to question whether God is really there for them.

Personally, I believe the classic Christian response to pain and suffering makes sense. The only way God could allow us to experience love, the greatest value in the universe, is if he gave us free will so we could choose whether or not to love him and others. Love *must* involve choice. Unfortunately, we've abused our freedom of choice by hurting each other, and that's where most of the world's suffering has come from.

Christian theology also provides an answer for the natural disasters that cause so much harm. As Cliffe Knechtle put it: "When we human beings told God to shove off, he partially honored our request." The result: creation was marred. We no longer live in the world as it was originally designed.

All of this, though, is an intellectual response. Yet Christianity offers so much more, because God himself set aside his exemption from pain and entered into human history, where he endured humiliation, rejection, torture, and death. "Our sufferings become more manageable in light of this," said British pastor John Stott. "There is still a question mark against human suffering, but over it we boldly stamp another mark, the cross which symbolizes divine suffering."

For Stott—and for me—belief in God would be repugnant if it weren't for the cross. "In the real world of pain," Stott said, "how could one worship a God who was immune to it?"

Chart It!

At this point in your spiritual journey, what do you believe about the problem of pain and suffering? On a scale from one to ten, place an X near the spot and phrase that best describes you. Share your selection with the rest of the group and give reasons for placing your X where you did.

1	2	3	4	5	6	7	8	9	10
I'm convinced that God is ultimately responsible for pain and suffering.				I'm unsure why God would allow pain and suffering.				I'm convinced that pain and suffering is the result of mankind's rejection of God.	

Study It!

Take some time later this week to check out what the Bible teaches about the problem of pain and suffering.

- ✦ Job 5:7
- ✦ Job 13:15
- ✦ Isaiah 43:2
- ✦ John 9
- ✦ John 16:33
- ✦ Romans 5
- ✦ Romans 8:12–30
- ✦ 2 Corinthians 4:16–18
- ✦ Ephesians 6:10–20
- ✦ James 1:2–18

SESSION 3

The
Mystery
of the *Trinity?*

Read It!

Three in One?

Mrs. Lundquist held a hard-boiled egg in front of her sixth-grade Sunday school class. "So, what is this?" she asked.

"Silly Putty!" Dan shouted. Most of the girls giggled. Ted punched him and muttered, "Shut up."

Kate whispered to Ted, "Jesus wouldn't want you to say 'shut up.'"

"Class," Mrs. Lundquist continued, "somebody please tell me what I'm holding up. Maybe somebody ate one of these this morning before coming to church?"

"We had Pop-Tarts," Carolyn responded. "But that's an egg."

Mrs. Lundquist smiled. "Yes, thank you, Carolyn. It's an egg, and this egg is going to demonstrate an important aspect of God: the Trinity."

"That's the Father, Son, and Holy Spirit," Carolyn stated proudly.

"You're right, Carolyn," Mrs. Lundquist affirmed. "The Trinity is a word we use to explain a truth about God: that he exists as three persons in one being. Three distinct persons, but only one God."

"That doesn't make sense," Ted interjected.

"Well, that's why I brought this egg to class this morning," Mrs. Lundquist said. "With the help of this egg and a little imagination, I'd like to try to explain to you the concept of the Trinity. You see, an egg is one thing, right?" The kids nodded, all except Ted, who stared with his head tilted to one side, watching, thinking. "This part I'm tapping, what is it called?"

"The shell," several kids responded.

"Exactly. Is the shell by itself an egg?"

"No," the class said in unison, with Ted still pondering silently.

"Okay, now I'm going to crack it open. See this part? It's called something ..."

"The white!"

"Exactly. Is the white of the egg the whole egg?"

"No!" They were on a roll now.

"Okay, now inside the white there's yet another part to this egg. What's the yellow part called?"

"The yolk!"

"Right! Is the yolk the egg?"

"No!"

"So to have an egg—one complete egg—we need all of these parts together. Three parts, all distinct with special qualities of their own, but united as one. This is an illustration of what God is like, you see." She began pointing to the parts of the egg. "God the Father, God the Son, God the Holy Spirit." She pulled out another egg. "Together," she concluded, holding the unbroken egg high in the air, "they are one."

Some of the kids nodded solemnly, as if they captured the complexity of the Trinity in that instant. Some restlessly watched the clock. Ted, however, still stared at the egg. "That doesn't explain it," he answered. "That doesn't explain anything."

"What?" Mrs. Lundquist looked toward him, slightly flustered, bringing the unbroken egg down, almost cradling it. "You say you don't understand it?"

"It just doesn't make sense to me," Ted answered. "You have to add up all three parts of the egg to make it an egg, but you don't add up the Father, Son, and Holy Spirit to make God. Aren't they all supposed to be God themselves?"

Mrs. Lundquist was taken aback. *Hmmmm*, she thought to herself, *he's right—the egg analogy is a bit, well ... scrambled.* She looked at the clock. There wasn't much time to spare.

"Okay, Ted, you've got a point there," she said. Ted smiled—a little too broadly, she thought to herself. "Let's try another approach. I know you've been a good student in school, so you probably know a few things about science." Ted nodded confidently. "Well," she continued, "you might remember something about the qualities of H_2O, then."

Carolyn held up her hand. "H_2O is water."

"That's right, Carolyn," Mrs. Lundquist continued, but she was zeroing in on Ted. "Water is the liquid form of H_2O, but what other forms can it take?"

"Ice!" said Kate.

"Yes, ice, frozen water, a solid. What else?"

"Steam," Ted said.

"That's right," Mrs. Lundquist nodded. "H_2O can also be in the form of steam or vapor. Is water vapor H_2O?"

"Yes," Ted said.

"Is ice still H_2O?" she asked.

"Yes," Ted answered.

"And what about liquid water?"

"Yes, that's still H_2O," he stated.

"Do you understand it, then, Ted? Three forms or expressions, each distinct and individual, but each equally H_2O. Do you see how that can help explain God in three persons, God the Father, God the Son, and God the Holy Spirit, yet as one being?"

The class was quiet except for the soft scrape of someone's shoe against the leg of a chair. Sunday school classes throughout the building would all be dismissed in seconds. "What do you think, Ted?" Mrs. Lundquist pressed. "Does that help explain the Trinity to you?"

Ted furrowed his brow. "Well, not exactly," he said slowly as he continued to think about the analogy. "H_2O can't be liquid, water, and gas at the same time. So are you saying that God takes on different forms as the Father, Son, and Holy Spirit at different times? Now he's the Father, then—*poof!* Now he's the Son?"

Mrs. Lundquist's eyes got wide. "Oh, no, I'm not saying that," she said. "All three persons of the Trinity exist simultaneously—that means at the same time. God doesn't morph from one form to the other."

"Then I don't think H_2O is a very good illustration either," Ted concluded. "In fact, what if there is no such thing as three forms of God in one?" He paused when Kate gasped. "Or," he continued, "maybe it just wasn't supposed to be explained in the first place. Maybe God wants to be harder to understand than an egg yolk, or an ice cube. Maybe he wants to stay a mystery."

The bell rang, and the classroom emptied before Mrs. Lundquist could say, "Have a good week." *Maybe*, she mused as she leaned against the wall, *the Trinity is a mystery after all.*

Watch It!

Use the following space to take notes as you view the video in which Lee Strobel interviews Rabbi Tovia Singer, a radio host on Israel national radio and author of the book *Let's Get Biblical*, and Dr. William Lane Craig, a research professor of philosophy at the Talbot School of Theology and author of numerous books, including *Reasonable Faith* and *Philosophical Foundations for a Christian Worldview.*

Discuss It!

1 What do you believe about God? Is there one God, no God, many gods, or one God in three persons? How is your *current* belief about God similar or dissimilar to what you believed when you were growing up?

2 How would you define the Trinity? In your definition, are the Father, Son, and Holy Spirit equals or is there a hierarchy? Are the Father, Son, and Holy Spirit three *different* gods or three persons of the *same* God all wrapped up in one? What are the respective roles of the Father, Son, and Holy Spirit?

3 William Lane Craig explains that God the Father, God the Son, and God the Holy Spirit are three distinct persons, but all equally God with three different roles. In what ways does this explanation make sense to you and in what ways does it not make sense?

> "The word 'Trinity,' first used in its Greek form *trias* by Theophilus of Antioch (circa AD 180), is not found in Scripture, but the conception is there both implicitly and explicitly."
>
> **F. L. Cross**

4 What do the following verses from the Old and New Testaments teach about the nature of God and Jesus Christ? On what points do they agree or disagree?

Old Testament

"I am the first and I am the last; apart from me there is no God.... You are my witnesses. Is there any God besides me? No, there is no other Rock; I know not one." (Isaiah 44:6, 8)

"I am the LORD, and there is no other; apart from me there is no God. I will strengthen you, though you have not acknowledged me, so that from the rising of the sun to the place of its setting men may know there is none besides me. I am the LORD, and there is no other." (Isaiah 45:5–6)

"Turn to me and be saved, all you ends of the earth; for I am God, and there is no other." (Isaiah 45:22)

For to us a child is born, to us a son is given, and the government will be on his shoulders. And he will be called Wonderful Counselor, Mighty God, Everlasting Father, Prince of Peace. (Isaiah 9:6)

He was despised and rejected by men, a man of sorrows, and familiar with suffering. Like one from whom men hide their faces he was despised, and we esteemed him not. Surely he took up our infirmities and carried our sorrows, yet we considered him stricken by God, smitten by him, and afflicted. But he was pierced for our transgressions, he was crushed for our iniquities; the punishment that brought us peace was upon him, and by his wounds we are healed. (Isaiah 53:3 – 5)

Then Isaiah said, "Hear now, you house of David! Is it not enough to try the patience of men? Will you try the patience of my God also? Therefore the Lord himself will give you a sign: The virgin will be with child and will give birth to a son, and will call him Immanuel." (Isaiah 7:13 – 14)

Hear, O Israel: The LORD our God, the LORD is one. (Deuteronomy 6:4)

New Testament

There is one body and one Spirit — just as you were called to one hope when you were called — one Lord, one faith, one baptism; one God and Father of all, who is over all and through all and in all. (Ephesians 4:4 – 6)

[Jesus answered,] "I and the Father are one."..."We are not stoning you for any of these," replied the Jews, "but for blasphemy, because you, a mere man, claim to be God." (John 10:30, 33)

"The most important one," answered Jesus, "is this: 'Hear, O Israel, the Lord our God, the Lord is one.'"..."Well said, teacher," the man replied. "You are right in saying that God is one and there is no other but him." (Mark 12:29, 32)

Thomas said to [Jesus], "My Lord and my God!" (John 20:28)

"Therefore go and make disciples of all nations, baptizing them in the name of the Father and of the Son and of the Holy Spirit."

Matthew 28:19

47

Watch It!

Use the following space to take notes as Lee Strobel continues to interview Rabbi Tovia Singer and Dr. William Lane Craig.

Discuss It!

5 Dr. Craig claims that the Old and the New Testaments are equally inspired by God, while Rabbi Singer contends that only the Old Testament is inspired by God. What do you think? Explain your response.

6 Lee Strobel points out that there are four clear teachings in the New Testament: (1) the Father is God, (2) the Son, Jesus, is God, (3) the Holy Spirit is God, and (4) there is only one God. If it could be substantiated that the Bible does in fact make these four claims, to what extent would that be sufficient evidence to conclude that God is triune? Why or why not?

> "God the Father is fully God. God the Son is fully God. God the Holy Spirit is fully God. The Bible presents this as fact. It does not explain it."
>
> **Billy Graham**

7 Rabbi Singer believes that the Holy Spirit is the dynamic presence of God but not a separate person. What do you believe about the Holy Spirit? According to the following verses from the Old and New Testaments, what does the Bible teach about the Holy Spirit?

> *Now the earth was formless and empty, darkness was over the surface of the deep, and the Spirit of God was hovering over the waters. (Genesis 1:2)*

> *The Spirit of God has made me; the breath of the Almighty gives me life. (Job 33:4)*

> *But it is the spirit in a man, the breath of the Almighty, that gives him understanding. (Job 32:8)*

> *If it were his intention and he withdrew his spirit and breath, all mankind would perish together and man would return to the dust. (Job 34:14–15)*

> *Now the Lord is the Spirit, and where the Spirit of the Lord is, there is freedom. (2 Corinthians 3:17)*

> *Because you are sons, God sent the Spirit of his Son into our hearts, the Spirit who calls out, "Abba, Father." (Galatians 4:6)*

> *But when he, the Spirit of truth, comes, he will guide you into all truth. (John 16:13)*

"By saying God has one essence and three persons it is meant that he has one 'What' and three 'Whos.' The three Whos (persons) each share the same What (essence). So God is a unity of essence with a plurality of persons. Each person is different, yet they share a common nature."

Norman Geisler, PhD

8 Rabbi Singer contends that Jesus isn't the Son of God, which Dr. Craig refutes. What do you think? Is Jesus the Son of God or not? Give reasons for your response.

9 What reasons can you give that support the idea that Jesus was God? What reasons can you give that support the idea that Jesus was not God?

10 Dr. Craig points out that one of the most rapidly growing segments of Judaism is Messianic Judaism, fully Jewish people who decide to place their belief and trust in Jesus as Messiah. These are strict monotheistic Jews who have become convinced that Jesus is the God who fulfills their Hebrew faith. Why do you suppose these people are changing their minds about the nature of Jesus and God?

Watch It!   *Lee's Perspective*

There's no question about it—the Trinity is not an easy concept to grasp. Perhaps it's no mistake that while the Bible freely uses various metaphors to illuminate its theology, nowhere does it offer an illustration to describe the Trinity. Indeed, it's a concept so sophisticated that it defies simple analogies.

Theologian Paul Enns doesn't even particularly like the word itself, because it stresses the three persons and not the unity within the Trinity. He prefers a German word that means "three-oneness." Still another descriptive word is "Triunity." In fact, the difficulty of coming up with an appropriate label is just one more illustration of how complicated God's nature really is.

Frankly, that shouldn't surprise us. The God who created the universe and who sustains it day by day is bound to be far beyond our mortal ability to fully understand. To me, the key remains this: does the Bible clearly communicate that the Father is God, that Jesus is God, and that the Holy Spirit is God? And does it emphatically declare that there is one God?

The answer to both those questions is yes. We can wrestle with trying to comprehend the Trinity, but if the Bible is accurate, then we can't ignore the fact that the Trinity is true. And contrary to some claims, it's not a contradiction.

Says theologian Norman Geisler: "The Trinity is not the belief that God is three persons and only one person at the same time and in the same sense. That would be a contradiction. Rather, it is the belief that there are three persons in one *nature*. This may be a mystery, but it is not a contradiction. That is, it may go beyond reason's ability to comprehend completely, but it does not go against reason's ability to apprehend consistently."

Chart It!

At this point in your spiritual journey, what do you believe about the Trinity? On a scale from one to ten, place an X near the spot and phrase that best describes you. Share your selection with the rest of the group and give reasons for placing your X where you did.

1	2	3	4	5	6	7	8	9	10
I'm not convinced that God the Father, God the Son, and God the Holy Spirit are three distinct persons, all equally God with three different roles.				I'm unsure what I believe about the Trinity.					I'm convinced that God the Father, God the Son, and God the Holy Spirit are three distinct persons, all equally God with three different roles.

Study It!

Take some time later this week to check out what the Bible teaches about the Trinity.

+ Isaiah 9:1–7
+ Isaiah 43:10–13
+ Isaiah 45:4–6, 18, 22
+ Isaiah 52:13–53:12
+ John 1
+ John 10
+ John 20:24–31
+ Ephesians 1:11–14
+ 1 Timothy 2:5

SESSION
4

Do Christians and *Muslims Worship* the *Same God?*

Read It!

No Difference?

David carefully compared the rows and rows of bottled water. It was hard to read the small print on the labels, but as far as he could tell, all the brands looked pretty much the same.

"Seems like they're identical," he concluded aloud as he tossed a case into his cart, "except for price. And I'll bet the lower priced ones actually taste better. Besides, for all I know, they're all probably made at the same plant using different labels."

"Yes, it's true, they do that," whispered an elderly woman standing nearby, clutching a wad of coupons in her left hand. "I always buy generic whenever I can. There's really no difference."

On his way home, he stopped by the drugstore to pick up some cold medicine his wife needed. He had some extra time to ask the pharmacist for some expert advice about which brand to go with. "It really doesn't matter, sir. If you read the ingredients you'll see that they're all basically the same." David was surprised to hear the pharmacist's explanation and grabbed the brand they'd always used before.

Back in his car, David heard a radio advertisement for a mortgage refinancing deal. *Wow, those rates are low*, he thought, *I better hurry up and call before I miss out on a chance for a sweet deal to lower our monthly payments.* As he jotted down the phone number he had second thoughts. *Then again, why bother? I might as well stick with the mortgage company I have now—I'm sure they'll be able to get me the same mortgage rates advertised here.*

When David was finally home, a colleague from work called. "What do you think about the buyout they announced today?"

"I doubt if things will be that different," David replied. "In the end, the new corporation will want us to do the same things we've always been doing. That's why they bought us—they know we're good at what we do. After they change the logo on the letterhead, our lives will be about the same as they've always been. We'll show up at meetings and hit our usual quotas and deadlines as best we can."

After dinner, David turned on the news channel. In a special religion segment, the reporter compared some of the beliefs and practices of various world religions. Christianity, Judaism, Islam, Buddhism, and Hinduism were each highlighted. Representatives from each of those religions were interviewed at length, asked similar questions about their understanding of God, the after-life, and truth sources. The segment showed various scenes of the faithful from each religion assembling at services, each in their own way.

David's wife turned to him. "I don't know why the reporter is only focusing on their differences," she said. "Why not concentrate on their similarities? After all, aren't they all worshiping the same God?"

David paused for a moment as the reporter gave her conclud-ing remarks. "I don't know," he said, "but it seems like every-where you turn, things appear to be different at first, but in the end, they're pretty much the same."

A shampoo commercial came on during the break. "Yes, I'll bet you're right," he added, "I'll bet they're all worshiping the same God after all."

Watch It!

Use the following space to take notes as you view the video in which Lee Strobel interviews Deborah Caldwell, a Christian and senior religion producer at the multifaith website beliefnet.com; Hesham A. Hassaballa, a physician, Muslim columnist for beliefnet.com, and author of the forthcoming book *The Beliefnet Guide to Islam*; and Ergun Caner who was raised as a Muslim but converted to Christianity in 1982. He currently teaches church history at Liberty University and wrote the award-winning book *Unveiling Islam* as well as *Christian Jihad*, which provides a provocative look at the Christian crusades.

Discuss It!

1 How do you feel about the fact that people believe so differently—and strongly—when it comes to religion? What reasons can you give for these differences?

2 Do you think it's important to keep an open dialogue going with people from different religious beliefs and backgrounds, or is it better to avoid these conversations altogether? What are the advantages and disadvantages of such a practice?

3 Deborah Caldwell expresses concern that the process of emphasizing religious differences causes unnecessary separation and division in our society. Do you agree? Why or why not? Do we all have to believe the same thing to get along?

> "There is no one alive today who knows enough to say with confidence whether one religion has been greater than all others."
> **Arnold Toynbee**

> "It was more than I could believe that Jesus was the only incarnate Son of God. And that only he who believed in him would have everlasting life. If God could have sons, all of us were his sons. If Jesus was like God ... then all men were like God and could be God himself."
>
> **Mohandas K. Gandhi**

4 What is your definition of *religious tolerance*? Does it mean that we should strive to identify ways religions are the same? Does it mean that we should never discuss religious differences? Does it mean that we should never hold to a belief system that excludes another belief system? Is *religious tolerance* a positive or negative term? Explain.

5 What's the difference between freedom *of* religion and freedom *from* religion? Which do you think should be the goal of a free society? Explain.

6 Explain the connection between the following:

- Build bridges of religious commonality
- Clearly define religious differences and similarities
- Openly discuss and acknowledge religious differences and similarities
- Seek to understand one another

Watch It!

Use the following space to take notes as Lee Strobel continues to interview Deborah Caldwell, Hesham A. Hassaballa, and Ergun Caner.

Discuss It!

7 Ergun Caner states that he is willing to fight for the freedom to believe whatever people choose to believe, but he is unwilling to let people redefine the God of the Bible into something inaccurate. Is this a reasonable expectation? Why or why not?

8 Hesham Hassaballa believes that the message from all the prophets throughout the ages was the same. Do you agree? Why or why not?

9 Do you think that Jews and Christians worship the same God? Why or why not?

> "Jesus was only a messenger of Allah.... Far is it removed from His transcendent majesty that [Allah] should have a son."
>
> **The Koran, Surah 4:171**

10 Consider the following list of core beliefs of Islam and Christianity. What are some significant similarities or differences between the two faiths?

Islam	Christianity
Allah is the one true God; there is no trinity (Father, Son, and Holy Spirit).	God is triune: one God in three persons (Father, Son, and Holy Spirit).
Allah is hidden and distant from humanity.	Christians worship and pursue a personal and loving relationship with God through Jesus Christ.
Jesus is one of many prophets of which Muhammad is superior. Jesus is Messiah, but not divine.	Jesus is God incarnate.
The Bible is inspired, but flawed; the Koran is superior to all other holy books.	The Bible, consisting of the Old and New Testaments, is the only divinely inspired, infallible source of truth.
The Koran teaches that Jesus never claimed to be God.	The Bible teaches that Jesus not only claimed to be God, but he proved it by dying on the cross and rising from the dead.
Abraham is the forefather of the faith through whom all the world will be blessed.	Abraham is the forefather of the faith through whom all the world will be blessed.

The soul is eternal and there will be a judgment day with a heaven and hell to follow.	The soul is eternal and there will be a judgment day with a heaven and hell to follow.
Jesus did not die for sin.	Jesus' death is the only payment for human sin; we must each individually accept this free gift to be saved.
Entrance into heaven is based on one's performance on earth and adherence to the five pillars of Islam.	Entrance into heaven is not based on performance but solely dependent on one's earthly relationship with Jesus Christ.

11 Do you think Muslims and Christians actually worship the same God, even though they may view or understand him differently? Explain.

12 Hassaballa believes Christians and Muslims worship the same God. Caner argues that the Muslim God is different from the Christian God because Muslims deny the deity of Jesus. Do you agree that this is a significant difference? Why or why not?

13 Hassaballa believes that Jesus was the Messiah but not the God-man. What's erroneous, if anything, about this belief? How is it possible for Jesus to be the Messiah without being the God-man? Do you agree with Caner that if Jesus was not God, his life and death were meaningless? Explain.

"I am the way and the truth and the life. No one comes to the Father except through me."

Jesus Christ, John 14:6

14 What is the basis for your beliefs, if any, about God? What would be sufficient to cause you to reconsider your beliefs and accept another faith?

Watch It! *Lee's Perspective*

I have a Muslim friend who comes over to my house. We grill steaks in the back yard and then we talk about faith. I tell him about the historical evidence that convinces me Christianity is true; he tells me why he disagrees and why he's an adherent of Islam. Sure, the discussion gets heated from time to time, but we don't pull out knives, attack each other, or belittle each other's beliefs. Through it all, we've remained friends.

Do we worship the same God? No, we don't. Take a look at the list of differences between Islam and Christianity included as part of this session. There are irreconcilable differences between the two. God cannot be triune and not triune at the same time. Jesus cannot be God's Son and a mortal messenger at the same time. God cannot be the intimate Father of Christianity and the distant and detached deity of Islam at the same time. Salvation cannot be solely through grace or be merited by good works at the same time.

However, I can be a Christian and still love my Muslim friend, as I trust he can remain my friend despite our differences. It would be wrong for us to paper over the distinctives of our faiths and pretend they say the same thing when they clearly don't. But it would be wrong, too, if we let our differences drive us to hatred or violence toward each other.

Truth should never be sacrificed on a false altar of religious tolerance. We can be civilized toward each other and still disagree, but my friend and I simply cannot be right at the same time. The laws of logic say it's impossible.

For me, the question is always this: where does the evidence point? Does it—or does it not—support the claim of Jesus that he's the sole pathway to God? My goal is to encourage everyone to make an informed decision about that topic.

So let me ask you: where do you stand right now on this paramount issue—and why?

Chart It!

At this point in your spiritual journey, what do you believe about the differences or similarities between Islam and Christianity? On a scale from one to ten, place an X near the spot and phrase that best describes you. Share your selection with the rest of the group and give reasons for placing your X where you did.

1	2	3	4	5	6	7	8	9	10
I'm convinced that Muslims and Christians worship the same God.				I'm unsure about whether Muslims and Christians worship the same God.				I'm convinced that Muslims and Christians do not worship the same God.	

Study It!

Take some time later this week to check out what the Bible teaches about the identity of God.

- Matthew 5:17–20
- Matthew 10:24–39
- John 3:16
- John 14:6–7
- Acts 4:12
- Hebrews 12:2
- 1 John 3:4–5
- 1 John 4:1–10

If you want to go deeper into the topics Lee introduced, get the complete story.

The Case for Christ

A Journalist's Personal Investigation of the Evidence for Jesus

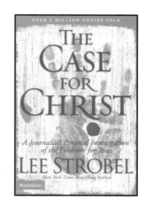

Is Jesus really the divine Son of God? What reason is there to believe that he is?

In his bestseller *The Case for Christ*, the legally trained investigative reporter Lee Strobel examined the claims of Christ by retracing his own spiritual journey, reaching the hard-won yet satisfying verdict that Jesus is God's unique son.

Written in the style of a blockbuster investigative report, *The Case for Christ* consults a dozen authorities on Jesus with doctorates from Cambridge, Princeton, Brandeis, and other top-flight institutions to present:

- Historical evidence
- Psychiatric evidence
- Other evidence
- Scientific evidence
- Fingerprint evidence

This colorful, hard-hitting book is no novel. It's a riveting quest for the truth about history's most compelling figure.

"Lee Strobel asks the questions a tough-minded skeptic would ask. Every inquirer should have it."

—Phillip E. Johnson, law professor, University of California at Berkeley

Hardcover 0-310-22646-5
Softcover 0-310-20930-7
Evangelism Pack 0-310-22605-8
Mass Market 6-pack 0-310-22627-9
Audio Pages® Abridged Cassette 0-310-24824-8
Audio Pages® Unabridged Cassette 0-310-21960-4
Audio Pages® Unabridged CD 0-310-24779-9

The Case for Faith
A Journalist Investigates the Toughest Objections to Christianity

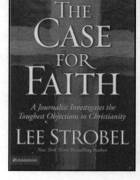

In his best-seller *The Case for Christ*, Lee Strobel examined the claims of Christ, reaching the hard-won yet satisfying verdict that Jesus is God's unique son.

But despite the compelling historical evidence that Strobel presented, many grapple with doubts or serious concerns about faith in God. As in a court of law, they want to shout, "Objection!" They say, "If God is love, then what about all of the suffering that festers in our world?" Or, "If Jesus is the door to heaven, then what about the millions who have never heard of him?"

In *The Case for Faith*, Strobel turns his tenacious investigative skills to the most persistent emotional objections to belief, the eight "heart" barriers to faith. *The Case for Faith* is for those who may be feeling attracted toward Jesus, but who are faced with formidable intellectual barriers standing squarely in their path. For Christians, it will deepen their convictions and give them fresh confidence in discussing Christianity with even their most skeptical friends.

Hardcover 0-310-22015-7
Softcover 0-310-23469-7
Evangelism Pack 0-310-23508-1
Mass Market 6-pack 0-310-23509X
Audio Pages® Abridged Cassettes 0-310-23475-1

Pick up a copy today at your favorite bookstore!

ZONDERVAN™

GRAND RAPIDS, MICHIGAN 49530 USA

WWW.ZONDERVAN.COM

"My road to atheism was paved by science . . . . But, ironically, so was my later journey to God."—Lee Strobel

The Case for a Creator:
A Journalist Investigates Scientific Evidence That Points Toward God

Lee Strobel, Author of
The Case for Christ *and*
The Case for Faith

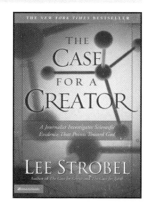

During his academic years, Lee Strobel became convinced that God was outmoded, a belief that colored his ensuing career as an award-winning journalist at the *Chicago Tribune*. Science had made the idea of a Creator irrelevant—or so Strobel thought.

But today science is pointing in a different direction. In recent years, a diverse and impressive body of research has increasingly supported the conclusion that the universe was intelligently designed. At the same time, Darwinism has faltered in the face of concrete facts and hard reason.

Has science discovered God? At the very least, it's giving faith an immense boost as new findings emerge about the incredible complexity of our universe. Join Strobel as he reexamines the theories that once led him away from God. Through his compelling and highly readable account, you'll encounter the mind-stretching discoveries from cosmology, cellular biology, DNA research, astronomy, physics, and human consciousness that present astonishing evidence in *The Case for a Creator*.

Hardcover: 0-310-24144-8
Unabridged Audio Pages® CD: 0-310-25439-6

ebooks:
Adobe Acrobat eBook Reader®: 0-310-25977-0
Microsoft Reader®: 0-310-25978-9
Palm™ Edition: 0-310-25979-7
Unabridged ebook Download: 0-310-26142-2

The Case for Easter
A Journalist Investigates the Evidence for the Resurrection

Lee Strobel

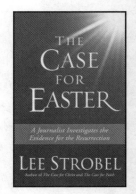

Did Jesus of Nazareth really rise from the dead?

Of the many world religions, only one claims that its founder returned from the grave. The resurrection of Jesus Christ is the very cornerstone of Christianity.

But a dead man coming back to life? In our sophisticated age, when myth has given way to science, who can take such a claim seriously? Some argue that Jesus never died on the cross. Conflicting accounts make the empty tomb seem suspect. And post-crucifixion sightings of Jesus have been explained in psychological terms.

How credible is the evidence for—and against—the resurrection? Focusing his award-winning skills as a legal journalist on history's most compelling enigma, Lee Strobel retraces the startling findings that led him from atheism to belief. Drawing on expert testimony first shared in his blockbuster book *The Case for Christ*, Strobel examines:

The Medical Evidence—Was Jesus' death a sham and his resurrection a hoax?

The Evidence of the Missing Body—Was Jesus' body really absent from his tomb?

The Evidence of Appearances—Was Jesus seen alive after his death on the cross?

Written in a hard-hitting journalistic style, *The Case for Easter* probes the core issues of the resurrection. Jesus Christ, risen from the dead: superstitious myth or life-changing reality? The evidence is in. The verdict is up to you.

Mass Market: 0-310-25475-2

The Case for Christmas
A Journalist Investigates the Identity of the Child in the Manger

Lee Strobel

Who was in the manger that first Christmas morning?

Some say he would become a great moral leader. Others, a social critic. Still others view Jesus as a profound philosopher, a rabbi, a feminist, a prophet, and more. Many are convinced he was the divine Son of God.

Who was he—really? And how can you know for sure?

Consulting experts on the Bible, archaeology, and messianic prophecy, Lee Strobel searches out the true identity of the child in the manger. Join him as he asks the tough, pointed questions you'd expect from an award-winning legal journalist. If Jesus really was God in the flesh, then there ought to be credible evidence, including

Eyewitness Evidence—Can the biographies of Jesus be trusted?

Scientific Evidence—What does archaeology reveal?

Profile Evidence—Did Jesus fulfill the attributes of God?

Fingerprint Evidence—Did Jesus uniquely match the identity of the Messiah?

The Case for Christmas invites you to consider why Christmas matters in the first place. Somewhere beyond the traditions of the holiday lies the truth. It may be more compelling than you've realized. Weigh the facts ... and decide for yourself.

Jacketed Hardcover: 0-310-26629-7

The Case for Faith
Visual Edition

Lee Strobel

Open this book and open your eyes. It is unlike any other you have held; a visual feast for your eyes and a spiritual feast for your soul. Lee Strobel, former atheist and award-winning legal editor of the *Chicago Tribune,* asks hard questions about God in *The Case for Faith* Visual Edition. And then he explores them with evidence from archaeology, history, and science—all set in powerful imagery and stunning typography. See the evidence for faith as you've never seen it before.

Softcover: 0-310-25906-1

Pick up a copy today at your favorite bookstore!

ZONDERVAN™

GRAND RAPIDS, MICHIGAN 49530 USA

WWW.ZONDERVAN.COM

God's Outrageous Claims
Discover What They Mean for You

Lee Strobel

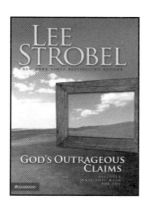

Lee Strobel presents thirteen phenomenal claims by God that can change the entire trajectory of your life and revolutionize your attitude, your character, and your relationships.

Take the Bible seriously and you'll discover that God makes some pretty amazing claims about you—and about what he wants to do in your life. *God's Outrageous Claims* examines important assertions that can transform your life into an adventure of faith, growth, and lasting fulfillment.

Discover how to grow in virtue, relate to others with authenticity, and make a real difference. *God's Outrageous Claims* is your guide to an exciting and challenging spiritual journey that can change you and your world profoundly.

Jacketed Hardcover: 0-310-26612-2

Pick up a copy today at your favorite bookstore!

GRAND RAPIDS, MICHIGAN 49530 USA

WWW.ZONDERVAN.COM

Tough Questions

Garry Poole and Judson Poling

> "The profound insights and candor captured in these guides
> will sharpen your mind, soften your heart, and inspire you and
> the members of your group to find vital answers together."
> —Bill Hybels

This second edition of Tough Questions, designed for use in any small group setting, is ideal for use in seeker small groups. Based on more than five years of field-tested feedback, extensive revisions make this best-selling series easier to use and more appealing than ever for both participants and group leaders.

Softcover

How Does Anyone Know God Exists? ISBN 0-310-24502-8

What Difference Does Jesus Make? ISBN 0-310-24503-6

How Reliable Is the Bible? ISBN 0-310-24504-4

How Could God Allow Suffering and Evil? ISBN 0-310-24505-2

Don't All Religions Lead to God? ISBN 0-310-24506-0

Do Science and the Bible Conflict? ISBN 0-310-24507-9

Why Become a Christian? ISBN 0-310-24508-7

Leader's Guide ISBN 0-310-24509-5

THE COMPLETE BOOK OF QUESTIONS

Garry Poole

Everyone has a story to tell or an opinion to share. *The Complete Book of Questions* helps you get the conversational ball rolling. Created especially for seeker small groups, these questions can jumpstart any conversation. They invite people to open up about themselves and divulge their thoughts, and provide the spark for stimulating discussions. This generous compilation of questions can be used in just about any context to launch great conversations.

Questions cover ten thematic categories, from light and easy questions such as "What room in your house best reflects your personality?" to deeper, more spiritual questions such as, "If God decided to visit the planet right now, what do you think he would do?" *The Complete Book of Questions* is a resource that can help small group leaders draw participants out and couples, friends, and families get to know one another better.

Softcover: ISBN 0-310-24420-X

We want to hear from you. Please send your comments about this book to us in care of zreview@zondervan.com. Thank you.

GRAND RAPIDS, MICHIGAN 49530 USA